P9-DHT-178

THE ADVENTURERS' HANDBOOK

AN EXTREME, EXTRAORDINARY, AND EXCITING
JOURNEY AROUND THE WORLD

By Anita Ganeri • Illustrated by Dusan Pavlic

FEIWEL AND FRIENDS • NEW YORK

Edited by Sally Pilkington

A FEIWEL AND FRIENDS BOOK
An Imprint of Macmillan

Library of Congress Cataloging-in-Publication Data Available

ISBN: 978-0-312-58090-2

Book design by Zoe Quayle

Originally published as *The Explorers' Handbook* in Great Britain by
Buster Books, an imprint of Michael O'Mara Books Limited

Feiwel and Friends logo designed by Filomena Tuosto

First U.S. Edition: 2010

10 9 8 7 6 5 4 3 2 1

www.feiwelandfriends.com

CONTENTS

GET SET TO EXPLORE THE WORLD

You are about to set off on an extraordinary adventure, exploring some of the most exciting places on Earth. You will be traveling across scorching deserts and frozen glaciers, climbing up active volcanoes and snow-capped mountains, plunging down raging rivers and beneath the surface of the planet's oceans. On the way, you will battle blizzards, survive hurricanes, and meet some amazing people. Planning ahead is essential to ensure all of your expeditions go without a hitch.

THE ADVENTURERS' PACKING LIST

The clothes and equipment you take will depend on where you are going and what you are planning to do when you get there. But whether you are exploring the poles, rain forests, deserts, or mountains, the basic essentials are the same. You need clothes to keep you warm and dry, and a wind- and rainproof shelter. You will need food and drink to keep you alive and give you the energy to enjoy your adventures. It is impossible to list everything you will need for every expedition, but here are some pointers to bear in mind when you are doing your packing.

ESSENTIAL EQUIPMENT

• Food—an emergency ration pack to keep you going for at least 24 hours.

8

• A water bottle and water-purifying tablets—tap water in some countries isn't always safe to drink, and natural disasters such as earthquakes and hurricanes can make water undrinkable.

• A place to sleep that is safe and warm—a sturdy tent, sleeping bag, and camping stove with matches (in a waterproof bag) or a lighter, so you can snuggle down and enjoy a hot meal after a long trek.

• The right clothes—you don't need to be a follower of fashion, but the right clothing can make or break an expedition.

• A good pair of walking boots—feet are the most reliable form of transport an explorer has, so look after them with a pair of good-quality walking boots.

• A map—knowing where you are is very important if you want to get where you are going. For this, you will need an up-to-date map and a compass.

• This book—do your research and know what to expect. It's the best preparation you can do.

Top tip: In case of an emergency, make sure you pack a first-aid kit, a flashlight, and extra batteries. You should also let people know where you are going before you leave and when you expect to be back.

HOW TO SAY "HELLO" AROUND THE WORLD

On your travels, you will meet people from many different parts of the world. Remember to treat all of them with respect and courtesy. Their local knowledge will make your trip so much more exciting, and could even save your life.

First impressions are very important, and what better way to greet the people you meet than being able to say hello to them in their own language. Smile, speak confidently, and you will soon have new friends from all over the globe. Here are some of the greetings you will need when you visit the places mentioned in this book.

Chinese	Ni hao
French	Bonjour
Hawaiian	Aloha
Hindi	Namaste
Inuit (Arctic Circle)	Kutaa
Italian	Buon giorno
Japanese	Konichi wa
Malagasy (Madagascar)	Salama

Mongolian	Sain baina uu
Norwegian	God dag
Portuguese	Bom dia
Russian	Zdravstvite
Sami (northern Norway)	Buorre beaivvi
Spanish	Hola
Swahili (Kenya and Tanzania)	Jambo
Tamasheq/Tuareg (Sahara Desert)	Ma d'tolahat

HOW TO BEAT JET LAG

As an explorer, you will travel great distances on your adventures—by foot, by boat, by camel, and also by plane. The globe is divided in segments—like an orange—into 24 different time zones. These time zones are what make it different times at different places on the planet. For example, when it is noon in London, England, it is 11 PM in Sydney, Australia, and 7 AM in New York City.

Flying around the world means you'll be crossing several different time zones in rapid succession and it can take your body a while to catch up. In the meantime, you may feel tired, weak, and disorientated for a while when you arrive at your destination. You may wake up too early in the morning, or want to fall asleep in the middle of the day. This is called "jet lag." Here are a few tips to help you cope when jet lag strikes.

• If you're traveling from west to east, go to bed earlier for a few nights before you leave. This gives your body time to adjust to your new time zone. If you're traveling from east to west, go to bed a few hours later.

• On the day of your journey, drink plenty of water—before, during, and after the flight. Being dehydrated can make jet lag worse.

• At the start of the flight, set your watch to the time it will be at your destination. Try to eat and sleep according to your watch. This will give you a head start settling into your new schedule.

• Try to get some exercise on the flight. Walk around the cabin to stretch your legs and stretch out your arms and shoulders while you are sitting in your seat.

• When you arrive, give yourself time to recover from the flight. It takes about a day to recover for each time zone you cross. Don't take a nap immediately, however tired you feel. Try to stay awake until bedtime.

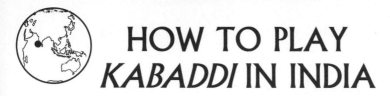

HOW TO PLAY
KABADDI IN INDIA

After a day chilling on the beaches of Goa, India, you need some exercise. You join a game of *kabaddi*—a fast and furious sport popular in India that you can also play in Pakistan, Iran, Japan, and Bangladesh if you happen to be passing through.

KABADDI RULES

There are two teams of 12 players—seven playing and five in reserve. Each team lines up on their side of the 13.5 yard by 11 yard court.

One team attacks. They send a player, called the "raider," into their opponents' half. The raider's job is to "tag" as many opponents as possible by touching them. The tagged players will be "out," if they can't stop the raider from making it back to his half. The difficult part is that the raider has to do all this in one breath, while chanting "Kabaddi! Kabaddi! Kabaddi!" He must return "home"

before his breath runs out. The word *kabaddi* is the Hindi word meaning "holding a breath."

Meanwhile, the defenders try to catch the raider. Their job is to hold the raider and stop him returning home before his breath runs out. If they manage, the raider is out, but if they don't, the defenders that have been tagged will be out.

During play, if a person goes over the boundary lines of the court or any part of his body touches the ground outside the court, he will be out unless he is struggling with another player.

Each time a player is out, the other team wins a point. A bonus of two points is awarded if the whole of the opposing team is out. Players who have been sent off can only return to the court when their side scores points during a raid.

A game has two 20-minute halves (15 minutes for women) with a five-minute break in between. The team with the most points wins.

Top tip: *Kabaddi* isn't included in the Olympic Games yet, but you could start training for the next Asian Games.

Kabaddi!
Kabaddi!
Kabaddi!
Kaba...

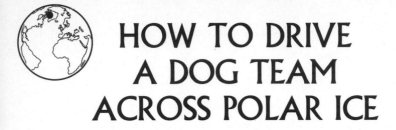

HOW TO DRIVE A DOG TEAM ACROSS POLAR ICE

You're on an Arctic expedition to study the effects of global warming on the thickness of the ice. The Arctic is the region at the northern end of the Earth, and the Arctic Ocean around the North Pole is entirely covered in ice—perfect for indicating a rise in the Earth's temperature.

By measuring the rate at which the ice is melting, scientists can work out the rate at which the Earth's temperature is increasing, as a result of global warming. Global warming is caused by humans pumping greenhouse gases, such as carbon dioxide and methane, into the atmosphere. These gases largely come from burning fossil fuels (oil, gas, and coal) in power stations, factories, and vehicles. Even a small rise in temperature is having a devastating effect on the Arctic, causing the ice to melt.

ARCTIC TRANSPORT

In order to get around on the polar ice in the Arctic, locals and explorers use dog sleds. Tiriaq is your local guide. He is an Inuit. The Inuit are the people who live closest to the Arctic Circle in Northwest Canada and Greenland. Tiriaq teaches you exactly how to hitch your dogs to your sled and use the right commands to control their every move. He has been driving dog sleds for years and explains the dos and don'ts of dog-sled driving.

DOGGY DOS AND DON'TS

1. Depending on the size of your sled, you'll need five to ten dogs. Siberian or Alaskan huskies are ideal, because they're strong, tough, and have super-thick fur coats to protect them from the cold.

2. Fit each dog with a chest harness, attached to the sled by a rope called a tugline. Hitch the dogs in a fan formation, which will ensure that the dogs spread out in a fan shape as they run.

This way, if one dog falls down a crevasse, the others don't get dragged down, as well. Let the most intelligent dogs take the lead—yes, dogs can be stupid or clever, too.

3. Get mushing (that's the technical term for driving a dog sled). Stand on the back of the sled and shout, "*Hike! Hike!*" to get the dogs moving. Other commands include:

> *Gee* which means "turn right"
> *Haw* which means "turn left"
> *Whoa* which means "stop."

4. Mushing takes lots of practice, so don't worry if you keep falling off in the beginning. The dogs will soon learn what you want them to do. To stop in an emergency, you can always push down on the brake bar at the back of the sled.

Top tip: To be a good musher, the dogs need to see you as the "leader of the pack." If you're nervous or hesitant, the dogs will become confused and won't respond to your commands.

HOW TO USE CHOPSTICKS IN CHINA

You're walking along the Great Wall of China—a giant wall built over 2,000 years ago that spans across the mountains of northern China. After a hard day's sightseeing, you're feeling hungry, so you go into a nearby restaurant to get something to eat. Not sure what to order, you decide to order a full banquet from the menu. Soon, plate after plate of steaming hot food begins arriving at your table. It looks and smells delicious, and you can't wait to dig in. The trouble is, when you reach for your knife and fork, you find only chopsticks on the table.

Chopsticks have been used in China for thousands of years, and they are still used in every restaurant and home today. Most chopsticks are made from wood or bamboo, and are square-sided, with a blunt end for picking up the food. They're called *kuai zi* in Chinese, which means "picker-uppers of small pieces."

TAKE CHARGE OF CHOPSTICKS

You decide to ask the couple sitting next to you how to eat with chopsticks and they happily offer to show you.

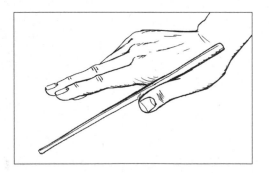

1. Place one chopstick in the space between your thumb and index finger.

2. Hold the chopstick in place by pushing it against the tip of your ring finger—the finger next to your little finger.

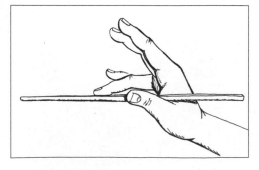

3. Hold the other chopstick between the tips of your index and middle fingers, a bit like holding a pencil (see opposite page). Use the tip of your thumb to keep the second chopstick secure.

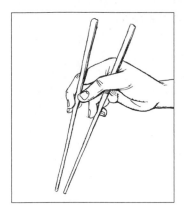

4. To pick up food, use your chopsticks like pincers. To do this, simply keep the bottom chopstick still while you move the top chopstick, using your index finger and thumb.

Top tip: Try to use chopsticks that can be reused or recycled. In China alone, about 45 billion pairs of wooden chopsticks are produced each year. That's the equivalent of 25 million trees.

TABLE MANNERS

The couple warn you, however, that there are a few rules about using chopsticks in public, so you listen carefully.

• Never use chopsticks to pass food from one person to another, unless they're having difficulty doing it themselves.

• Don't use a chopstick to spear food. Luckily for you, Chinese food is usually chopped up to make it easier to handle.

• Never lick your chopsticks at the dinner table.

• Don't wave your chopsticks around while you're talking about your travel adventures. This is considered very rude.

• Between mouthfuls, rest your chopsticks beside your bowl on a little block designed to keep the points off the table.

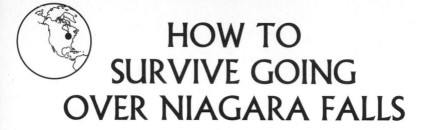

HOW TO SURVIVE GOING OVER NIAGARA FALLS

You're measuring the rate of soil erosion along the banks of the Niagara River above the Horseshoe Falls, a part of the Niagara Falls, which lie on the border between Canada and the U.S.

FALL FORMATION

Niagara Falls is the biggest waterfall in North America. It was formed as a result of huge glaciers moving northwards nearly 12,000 years ago, which caused water from Lake Erie to flow over a gigantic ridge known as the Niagara Escarpment.

The water is pushed over this ridge at such force that the soil on the ridge is steadily eroding, causing huge chunks of rock to break off and flow downstream. Your job is to monitor the rate at which the soil is eroding in order to help experts discover ways to slow it down.

Disastrously, you get spooked by what you think is the sound of a grizzly bear, and stumble and fall into the rushing torrent. Before you know it, you are speeding toward the edge of the falls. Niagara Falls might not be the highest waterfall in the world, but it plunges over a series of colossal cliffs in a swirling crash of icy-cold water and spray. To have any chance of surviving, you need to keep your cool.

SURVIVAL TIPS

In 1901, an American teacher, Anna Edson Taylor, age 63, strapped herself into a barrel and threw herself into the Falls. Astonishingly, she survived the drop without serious injury, apart from some cuts and bruises. Without a barrel, however, you will have little chance of survival without the advice below.

• Take the plunge. Just before you go over the Falls, throw yourself out and away from the edge. This will help to make sure you don't get trapped behind the curtain of water and run out of air.

• The safest way to descend is feet first, with your arms above your head. Squeeze your feet together and keep your body upright, as if you are standing to attention. Cover your head with your arms to protect it.

• Take a deep breath just before you reach the bottom of the drop and start swimming as soon as you hit the water—the water at the bottom of Horseshoe Falls is 185 feet deep, deeper than the falls themselves. Swimming will help stop you from sinking too far down, and it will also get you moving away from the waterfall and into safer water.

Luckily for you, you've fallen into the slightly less dangerous of Niagara's two waterfalls. Despite the American Falls being lower (at 70 feet, compared to Horseshoe's 174 feet), there is a nasty pile of rocks at the bottom from a massive landslide caused by the effects of the soil erosion you are studying—and these would make for a painful landing.

WARNING

Don't ever attempt to throw yourself off Niagara Falls on purpose. There is little chance you will survive to explore anywhere else in the world.

HOW TO RIDE A CAMEL ACROSS THE SAHARA

Phew! You're in the sweltering heat of the Sahara Desert, an enormous expanse of sand and rock that stretches across the top of North Africa. The temperature is reaching 130°F, and you are so thirsty you could drink a whole swimming pool. The Sahara Desert covers an area of nearly 5.5 million square miles, and your mission is to cross it without dying of heat, dehydration, or exhaustion.

DESERT TRANSPORT

Thankfully, a group of local Tuareg people are passing by and they take pity on you. The Tuareg are nomadic, which means they travel from place to place across the desert. They know the desert like the backs of their hands. A young boy introduces himself to you as

Azzad, and kindly asks you to join them. He even offers a spare camel for you to ride.

Camels are by far the most reliable means of desert transport. They're superbly adapted to the testing conditions and can go without food and water for many days. They can carry heavy loads (such as you and your belongings) for hundreds of miles without getting tired. Unfortunately for you, this camel doesn't look happy at the thought of giving you a ride.

Azzad senses you are nervous, so he offers to give you a lesson in camel riding to get you started on your expedition. You'll be riding a dromedary, which has only one hump. Camels with two humps are called Bactrian camels and are more at home in the Gobi and other deserts in Central Asia.

CAMEL COACHING

1. Mount your camel while it is sitting down. Stand on one leg and throw your other leg over the camel's hump. Make sure you will end up facing the camel's head, and not the other end. Sit down firmly in the saddle.

2. To make the camel stand up, hold the reins and shout "Up! Up!" You will feel as if you are about to be tipped off as the camel lunges forward, then back. Sit firmly in the saddle and you won't take a tumble.

3. Show your camel who is boss by holding the reins firmly, but without jerking or tugging them. Camels are intelligent animals and can sense if a rider is nervous or frightened.

4. When you want to stop and get off, shout "Koosh! Koosh!" to instruct your camel to sit down.

TOP TUAREG TIPS

• Keep your clothes on—even though your first instinct may be to strip down to your birthday suit to cool off. Bare skin will burn quickly in the hot sun. The Tuareg wear layers of loose cotton clothing to protect their skin and to keep the sweat close to their bodies, because this helps to conserve precious water.

• Avoid traveling during the hottest times of day—ride at night or during the early morning or evening. When the sun is at its highest, find shade and rest.

• Eat salty food—this will help replace the salt your body loses in your sweat. (Remember to stop eating salty food when you leave the desert, as too much salt can be very bad for you.)

• Look out for oases—these are places in the desert where you will be able to find shade and get plenty of water to drink.

• Keep an eye out for sandstorms. An approaching sandstorm looks like a dark cloud in the distance. Crouch down next to your camel or a large rock, and cover your eyes and mouth with sunglasses and a scarf.

HOW TO DIVE BELIZE'S BLUE HOLE

Wind is whipping through your hair as you speed across the turquoise ocean heading for a diving adventure. You're in a boat with a team of marine biologists, just off the coast of Central America in the country of Belize. You're heading for the Blue Hole, a perfectly circular sinkhole (a hole in the middle of a slab of rock), and one of the world's most exciting dive sites.

About a third of a mile across and 475 feet deep, the Blue Hole is located in the middle of the world's second largest coral reef. It gets its name from the color of its water, which is a dazzling shade of deep blue.

ICE AGE ACTION

Mike, a marine biologist with you on the expedition, explains that he dives the Blue Hole to study the animal life that lives around it. Before the last Ice Age (a period over 20,000 years ago, when the Earth was extremely cold, causing most of its water to freeze), the Blue Hole would have been on dry land, and was, in fact, a cave. When the Ice Age ended, the ice melted and the sea level rose, flooding the cave and causing its roof to collapse in the perfect circle seen today. There are sinkholes all over the world, but the Blue Hole is the biggest by far.

You've picked the best time to make your dive, since the sea is calm and visibility is good between April and June.

TAKING THE PLUNGE

1. The divers begin to put on their gear, so you do the same. First, you put on your wet suit and then your weight belt (this will help you to sink).

2. You then sit down at the edge of the boat and put on your fins. Don't attempt to walk around in them because you will be very unstable. Don't call them "flippers" either–experienced divers laugh at people who call fins flippers.

3. Put on your mask and snorkel so that your snorkel hangs down the left-hand side of your face.

4. Now, you put on your buoyancy control device or BCD. This is an inflatable life jacket that controls whether you float or sink–your tank of pressurized air will be strapped to the back.

5. Almost ready to go, you give one another's equipment a final check and signal "OK," by making the gesture shown here.

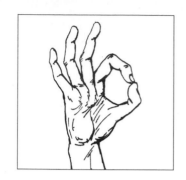

6. You fully inflate your BCD and put the mouthpiece, called the regulator, into your mouth, holding it in place using the palm of your right hand, while using your fingers to secure your mask. You then fall backward into the water.

7. Once everyone is in the water, you begin your descent.

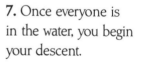

THAT SINKING FEELING

Looking down into the Blue Hole, you see a bottomless pit with plunging, sheer walls teeming with coral and colorful fish. At around 40 yards below the surface, you see stalactites hanging from the cave wall—some of them are thicker than tree trunks. You feel frightened as a shoal of reef sharks swims past you, but Mike signals "OK" to reassure you that these sharks are just nosy and that you are not in any danger.

After just eight minutes in the Blue Hole, your dive time is up. Mike gives you the thumbs-up to signal that it's time to head toward the surface. You very slowly begin your ascent. Surfacing too quickly can cause bubbles of nitrogen gas in your blood to expand, which can be very painful and even kill you. This is called the bends. To avoid this, Mike makes you perform something called a safety stop. Five yards before you reach the surface, Mike signals to stay at this depth for three minutes, which lets some of the nitrogen escape. After the three minutes is up, Mike gives you the thumbs-up and you head toward the surface.

WARNING

Diving the Blue Hole is an awesome experience, but it's also extremely dangerous and should only be tackled by experienced divers, never by a beginner.

HOW TO CROSS A GLACIER IN ARGENTINA

An icy-cold wind brings you to your senses. You are climbing in the Andes Mountains in Argentina. With you are Toby and Josefina, two expert climbers. The views are spectacular, but the climbing is hard work. You are looking forward to getting to camp for a well-earned rest, but you know the real test lies just ahead as you spot a gigantic glacier (an enormous slab of ice) that is blocking your way.

THE PERITO MORENO GLACIER

You have reached the majestic Perito Moreno Glacier, one of 48 glaciers in the Los Glaciares National Park. Like all glaciers, the Perito Moreno Glacier was created by snow falling high up in the mountains. Each year, more snow fell in the winter than could melt away in the spring and summer. Over time, as more and more snow fell, it turned into solid ice under its own weight. Eventually, this huge slab of ice got so heavy, it began to slide downhill. It is a whopping 19 miles long and up to 2 miles wide. Toby tells you that despite its enormous size, this glacier is moving—and moving fast—at a rate of about 6.5 feet a day.

You know that you are going to have to traverse the glacier—traverse is the technical term for crossing the slab of ice. Toby tells you that you have to listen to his advice because this can be very dangerous.

ESSENTIAL EQUIPMENT

Before you set off, Josefina explains some of the equipment you have with you for coping with this challenging environment.

• The glacier can get very steep in places and very slippery, so it is easy to lose your footing. This is why you have crampons, metal frames covered with sharp spikes, strapped to each of your climbing boots. On the glacier, you must try to keep as many spikes as possible in contact with the ice and make sure you dig them in as firmly as you can.

pick

• You also have an ice axe to hold onto. She explains that you should dig your axe into the ice as soon as you feel yourself falling, to stop yourself sliding downhill. This maneuver is called an ice-axe arrest.

HOW TO PERFORM AN ICE-AXE ARREST

As well as having the right equipment, it is important that you know how to use it. Josefina wants to see that you are prepared for the ice by showing you how to do an ice-axe arrest.

1. Your ice axe should be kept close at hand. When walking, hold your ice axe as you would a walking stick, in the hand facing uphill. Keep the sharp pick pointing behind you. Don't keep your axe strapped to your back since it won't be much use there.

2. As you fall, or when you are sliding, roll onto your front and bring the ice axe diagonally across your body quickly with the pick away from you. Stick the pick into the ice, and grab the spike in your other hand to stop it digging into you. Hold it next to your hip, pulling your elbows in to steady the axe.

3. As you are sliding, keep your knees bent and wide apart, and your feet up above the ice to stop your crampons sticking into the ice. Arch your back to keep your stomach off the ice–this puts more of your weight on the pick, making it easier to stop.

WALKING ON ICE

Before setting foot on the glacier, Toby ties one end of a 25-yard-long rope to the harness around his waist, and the other end to yours. Josefina does the same with a similar rope. She tells you that this is the safest way to travel across the glacier. Being tied together this way means that if one of you falls down a huge crack in the ice called a crevasse, the other two can haul the person out. Crevasses are caused by movements in the ice causing it to split open. Crevasses can be hundreds of yards deep, but are very difficult to spot when covered with snow.

Toby leads the way and you wait until the rope between you is almost taut. Josefina follows. You are careful to make sure that neither rope is too slack since this means someone could have a long way to fall. Slowly and carefully, you begin to make your way across the glacier.

When you arrive at the camp, there is a warm welcome. You are relieved that you didn't take a tumble on the glacier, and are very pleased when you are given a hot cup of cocoa to warm you up.

HOW TO SWIM THE ENGLISH CHANNEL

Dressed only in a bathing suit and covered from head to foot in thick, slimy grease, you are standing on Shakespeare Beach at Dover, England. The famous chalky White Cliffs along the coast rise up above your head as you prepare to swim the English Channel—the 21-mile-wide stretch of cold, choppy sea between England and France. You are heading to Cap Gris Nez in France, the shortest route across.

Swimming the Channel is the ultimate challenge for any swimmer. You've been training for months, and if you make it, you will take your place in the history books. Of the hundreds of people who attempt it each year, fewer than one in five manage to swim all the way.

TOP TRAINING TIPS

Luckily, you are in good hands. Your trainer, Len, has swum the Channel many times. Below is some of his essential advice.

• Start training several months beforehand in your local swimming pool. Gradually build up to swims that last for several hours.

• The water in the Channel is very cold at just 55–64°F, so you need to get used to swimming in cold water. Taking cold baths can help, as can swimming in the sea in winter, even if it's only for a few minutes. If your body isn't used to the cold, you run

the risk of suffering from a condition called hypothermia that can make you very ill, and even kill you.

• Get all the right equipment. According to the official rules, your swimsuit must not cover your arms or legs. You are allowed to wear goggles, a swimming cap, a nose clip, and ear plugs.

• Hire a boat to go with you. This is called a pilot boat and it stays next to you throughout the swim in case of emergency.

TAKING THE PLUNGE

Today is the day. The support team on your pilot boat have listened carefully to the weather forecast and it looks perfect—a clear sky with very little wind. Len warns you, however, that the conditions in the Channel can change suddenly, with gale-force winds, high waves, and thick fog a possibility.

You are covered in grease to keep you warm in the chilly water. The grease also helps stop parts of your body from chafing and feeling sore. You can use any kind of grease, such as goose fat, but swimmers usually use a mixture of petroleum jelly and lanolin (wool fat).

You walk into the water and start swimming. Front crawl is the best stroke to use because you can develop a steady pace, hopefully making it easier to keep swimming for hours on end.

Every hour, members of your support team pass you food and drink from the boat. They pass them over in bottles and bags on the ends of long poles or pieces of string.

After 11 hours and 32 minutes, you finally reach Cap Gris Nez and now you have to haul yourself onto the beach. The rules say that you must get out of the water for your crossing to count.* The world record for swimming the Channel is just under seven hours.

TAKE THE CHANNEL CHALLENGE

If you don't want to swim the Channel, you could see how far you would get by swimming in your local swimming pool. Each time you go swimming, keep a logbook of how many laps you do. You will have to swim an average 55-yard-length pool a whopping 670 times to have swum a distance equivalent to crossing the Channel—so, you had better get started soon.

---

*Two organizations observe and authenticate Channel swims. You can look at one set of rules at http://channelswimming.net.

HOW TO JUMP HIGH WITH THE MAASAI IN KENYA

On safari in Kenya, you get up close to elephants and zebras, and even get spotted by a pride of lions. As you head back to camp, you are also lucky enough to meet some Maasai warriors, dressed in their brilliant red robes. They invite you to come to their village for a special feast. The Maasai are a group of people that traditionally live as cattle herders, but they also have a reputation as brave warriors and athletic dancers.

Today they are performing their famous jumping dance (the Maasai call it *adumu*) and ask you to take part. This is a great honor and you want to do the best you can.

Top tip: The jumping dance is for boys only, so girls should not try to join in. It is part of a four-day-long ceremony that marks the start of the boys' adult lives. From now on, they are warriors whose job is to protect their families, herds, and community.

LET'S DANCE

1. Take your place in the line of warriors and form a circle with them. One warrior starts the singing and the rest of the warriors, including you, join in.

2. When your turn comes, go into the middle of the circle. Take a deep breath. Put your feet together, bend your knees, and jump straight up into the air. Keep your head high with your chin tipped up, and your shoulders back.

3. Keep jumping up and down, as high and straight as you can, without letting your heels touch the ground. The dance is designed to show off your strength and stamina, so the higher you go, the better. Make sure you bend your knees as you land so you don't hurt your legs.

4. Stop after four or five jumps, or when you are feeling tired. Let someone else have a turn while you get your breath back.

5. Keep practicing. It is doubtful that you will be able to jump higher than your Maasai friends; they practice for hours and are amazingly fit and strong.

HOW TO SURVIVE IF MOUNT ETNA ERUPTS

A strange rumbling sound fills the air. You are standing on the slopes of a mountain on the island of Sicily in Italy. Rather worryingly, you see steam pouring out of the mountain's peak. This is because Mount Etna is no ordinary mountain. It stands about 2 miles high, and is the biggest, most active volcano in Europe—and one of the most active volcanoes in the world. Mount Etna is often quiet for months on end, but the rumbling you hear may be a warning sign that the volcano is about to erupt.

ERUPTION!

Deep beneath Mount Etna, a mixture of gases and magma (rock so red-hot it has melted) is moving and expanding, causing pressure on the surrounding rocks to build. A point will come where this pressure can no longer be contained. This is when the magma and gases burst out through cracks in the ground—a volcanic eruption.

Every few years, Mount Etna erupts and sends great streams of lava (the name for magma once it reaches the surface) flowing down its slopes. The lava buries everything in its path, including houses and villages.

WARNING SIGNS

You can feel the ground starting to shake. Earthquakes often happen before an eruption. They signal that magma is beginning to move beneath your feet. Keep your eyes, ears, and even nose open for these warning signs.

• The side of the volcano may start to bulge or swell as the magma wells up below its surface.

• Look out for puffs of ash and steam coming from the crater, or from cracks on the volcano's slopes.

• Often you will be able to hear the volcano starting to stir. Listen for loud bangs, like gunshots, and hissing, roaring, and chugging sounds.

• Who farted? You may notice a smell like rotten eggs. This comes from a gas called hydrogen sulphide, which seeps up through cracks in the ground.

HOT TIPS

Watching an erupting volcano firsthand is exciting, but it can also be extremely dangerous—especially if the volcano explodes violently. Being well prepared is the best way to survive.

• If Mount Etna erupts while you are outside, try to get to higher ground so that you are out of reach of debris flowing downhill. Lava usually moves quite slowly, so you should be able to outrun it, but go carefully and never try to cross its path. You might fall in it and get badly burned or killed.

• Watch out for "bombs" (flying chunks of lava), hot ash, lava flows, and lahars (mudslides).

• The best place to be if a volcano blows is inside. Close all doors and windows. Put tape around the edges of drafty windows and stuff rolled-up towels under the doors to prevent ash and dust from getting in.

• Listen to the TV or radio for information and advice. Don't go outside until you are told that the eruption is over and it is safe.

• Make sure that you clear any fallen ash from the roof and gutters of your house. Volcanic ash is very heavy and its weight could bring your house crashing down on you.

HOW TO CRACK A COCONUT ON A DESERT ISLAND

You are sailing across the Pacific Ocean when disaster strikes. Your ship runs aground on a coral reef and you find yourself marooned on a desert island. You're alone on a sandy beach with nothing but swaying coconut palms for company. Although some of your precious provisions have washed up with you, you aren't sure how long it will be until you are rescued, so you will need to make them last as long as you can.

Feeling hungry, you pick up a coconut with a hard, hairy shell. Here's how to crack your coconut open to get to the delicious white "meat" inside.

1. Pull off the hairy outer layer called the "husk."

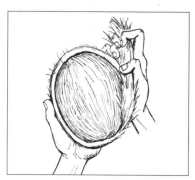

2. Look at the coconut carefully. At one end, you will see three dents that look like two eyes and a mouth.

3. Hold that end of the coconut firmly in one hand. Find the "seam" or "rib" that runs between the two eyes. Follow the seam to the middle of the coconut. Then imagine a line running around its fattest part.

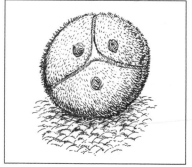

4. Take a large rock in your other hand and give the coconut a few good, hard taps along this line. Keep turning the coconut so you hit it all the way around. After a few whacks, the coconut should break into two halves.

5. Scrape out the white "meat" inside with a sharp shell or piece of rock. Smell the inside of the coconut before you eat it. If it smells sour or moldy, throw it away and get another one.

Top tip: Don't throw the halves of the coconut shell away. Use one to collect coconut water from your next nut. Push a sharp stick through two of its eyes. Drain the coconut water that's inside into your shell cup.

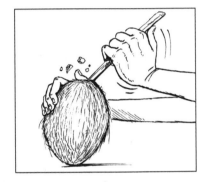

HOW TO BUILD A SNOW HOLE IN THE ARCTIC

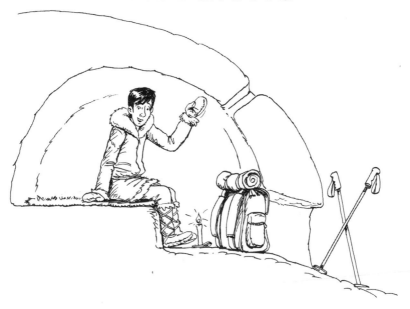

For miles around, all you can see is an expanse of dazzling white. It's freezing and the snow is falling thick and fast. You are on a hunting trip in the Arctic in the icy far north of Canada. Your guides are two local Inuit hunters (see page 17), called Ituko and Irniq, and they are taking you to find seals, walruses, and caribou.

INUIT LIFESTYLE

Traditionally, the Inuit were nomads, traveling across the frozen land, hunting for the animals they lived on. Essential skills, handed down, allowed them to survive in their hostile environment.

In the winter, the Inuit lived in homes dug into the ground for warmth. In the summer, they moved to tents made from seal or caribou skins. Today, most Inuit live in wooden houses in small towns and villages with modern facilities, such as running water and central heating. Fortunately for you, there are still some Inuit around, including your two guides, who haven't forgotten their snow survival skills.

As you're traveling, the falling snow is getting heavier. You need to find shelter, fast. You can find nothing to use but ice and snow, so you turn to your guides for help. Thankfully, they don't seem worried. The Inuit have been building warm, waterproof shelters out of snow for centuries. Ituko tells you that there's not enough time to build an igloo from blocks of hard snow. Instead, your two guides show you how to build yourself a snow hole—a simpler shelter that will keep you warm and dry until you're able to continue with the hunt.

CONSTRUCTING YOUR SNOW HOLE

1. First you need to find the right spot to dig your shelter in the snow. Irniq explains that a slope, or a deep drift of snow, is the best possible location for shelters like these because you can tunnel into them easily. Make sure that the snow above your chosen slope isn't too soft or likely to avalanche on top of you. Pick a point where the entrance to your snow hole will be out of the wind.

2. Using a snow shovel, dig a tunnel of about a yard in length into the snow.

3. Once you're a yard into the snow, you can start to hollow out the snow to create a small chamber at the end of your tunnel. This "room" should be big enough to fit you and all your equipment inside it, and tall enough for you to sit up straight comfortably. The walls and roof must be at least 2 feet thick.

4. Use some of the snow leftover from digging your chamber to create a "sleeping platform," which is a ledge above the floor. It will be warmer on the ledge, as freezing cold air is heavier than cool air and will collect at the bottom of the chamber.

5. Mark the top of your shelter with something obvious, so that other travelers can spot your snow hole and find you easily— crossed ski poles are perfect for this.

6. Once you have all your belongings inside your chamber, position your backpack in the entrance tunnel to keep out some of the cold air. Make sure you sleep with your shovel close at hand, just in case you need to dig yourself out.

7. Poke a hole through the roof of your shelter for ventilation, in case you want to have candles burning, or light a small stove.

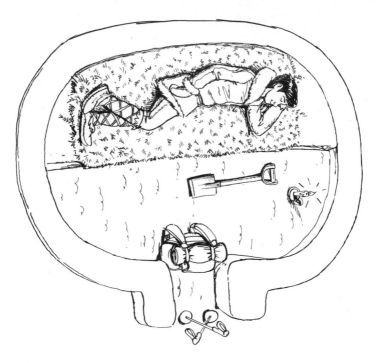

8. Spread some animal skin or your sleeping bag over the platform for extra insulation.

9. Smooth the walls and ceiling of your little sleeping chamber to stop water dripping on you as your body heat warms up the snow.

You now have a snow shelter that will keep you safe and warm until the blizzard outside has passed.

HOW TO TRACK A TWISTER IN TORNADO ALLEY

It's late in the afternoon at the beginning of summer, and the air is hot and dusty. You are in a pickup truck with a group of filmmakers and scientists known as storm chasers, in a part of the Midwest known as Tornado Alley. Storm chasers travel all over this region looking for tornadoes in order to film them and measure the violent winds they cause.

Tornado Alley stretches across the states of Texas, Oklahoma, Kansas, Nebraska, and North and South Dakota. It is a must-see for budding storm chasers as over 800 tornadoes, or twisters, strike this region each year.

LET'S TWIST

As the sky darkens and begins to look more menacing, you feel the wind pick up. All of a sudden, there is a mighty rumble of thunder followed quickly by a flash. A filmmaker called Chet tells you this means that there is a good chance you will see a tornado.

Tornadoes form beneath thunderstorms. Wind above the storm moves more quickly than the air lower down. This causes the storm to spin. As it begins to spin faster, a funnel forms at the center where the air is spinning at its fastest. As this funnel spins, it sucks up more and more air from below the storm, growing longer and longer until it meets the ground.

When twisters touch down on the ground, they leave a trail of destruction behind them. They can smash up houses, pick up cars and trains, and even lift fish from lakes, dumping them miles away. Worse still, they may last for several hours with winds reaching 300 miles per hour. Tornadoes can travel hundreds of miles before running out of energy.

MEASURING TORNADOES

In the distance, a funnel-shaped twister starts whirling down menacingly from a greenish-black thundercloud. Chet starts his camera and tries to capture as much of the storm as he can. His friend, Kaitlyn, attempts to measure the wind speed, but says that the winds are too strong for her instruments. For this reason scientists rate tornadoes according to the damage they cause, using a scale called the Enhanced Fujita Scale.

THE ENHANCED FUJITA SCALE

Scale	Wind speed	Possible damage
EF0	40–72 miles per hour	**Light damage.** Lifts surface slightly from roofs; damages gutters; breaks branches from trees.
EF1	73–112 miles per hour	**Moderate damage.** Roofs stripped; mobile homes overturned; glass windows broken.
EF2	113–157 miles per hour	**Considerable damage.** Tears off roofs; destroys mobile homes; uproots large trees; lifts cars off ground.
EF3	158–207 miles per hour	**Severe damage.** Whole houses destroyed; trains overturned; bark stripped from trees; heavy cars lifted from ground.
EF4	208–260 miles per hour	**Devastating damage.** Whole houses completely flattened; cars hurled through the air.
EF5	261–318 miles per hour	**Total destruction.** Houses swept away; high-rise buildings badly damaged; car-sized debris flung through the air.

TORNADO SAFETY WARNING

Storm chasing can be very exciting, but it is very dangerous and should only be attempted with a team of experts. Never try and chase a storm yourself. If a tornado is heading your way, you need to take action—fast.

WHAT TO DO

1. Get indoors and put as many walls between you and the wind outside as possible. Stay away from windows and doors. In Tornado Alley, many houses have storm shelters in their cellars and these are the safest places to head for.

2. If you haven't got a storm shelter, get to the lowest possible part of the building or go to the bathroom and get into the tub. Hide under a mattress, soft blankets, or pillows to protect yourself from flying debris.

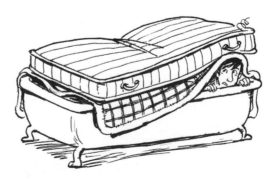

3. If you are unlucky enough to be caught outside, you might have to hide in a ditch or lie flat, facedown, on the ground. This is not ideal, but it may protect you from high winds and debris. Keep as far away from trees and cars as possible. Use your arms to cover your head and neck, and don't be tempted to look around you to see what's happening as the twister hits.

4. Don't try to sit the storm out in a car. The winds inside the twister can reach speeds of more than 300 miles per hour, which is certainly strong enough to pick up your car and hurl it down the road with you inside.

> **Top tip:** Never try to outrun a twister on foot.
> It can travel far faster than you can.

HOW TO AVOID A SEA WASP IN AUSTRALIA

You are snorkeling off the north coast of Australia. The sun is shining and the water is wonderfully warm and calm. Beautiful fish are all around you. A few yards away, you see a large, squarish, pale-blue jellyfish floating like a ghost. Beware—this is a sea wasp, otherwise known as a box jellyfish, and you should avoid it at all costs.

A sea wasp has around 60 tentacles that can be up to 3 yards long. Each tentacle is loaded with thousands of stinging cells, designed to kill prey instantly. Sea wasps are among the world's deadliest creatures; their poison can kill someone in just three minutes. The pain alone is enough to send people into shock and cause them to drown.

You decide it is best not to risk staying in the water and head back to shore. Sea wasps are one of the few jellyfish that can travel without relying on drifting in the current, so you want to be well out of the way in case it decides to head toward you.

FIRST AID

Phew! That was a lucky escape, but there are still jellyfish out there. If someone does get stung, call an ambulance immediately and while you are waiting, pour vinegar over the stings. The acid in the vinegar stops the sea wasp's stings from working and will ease the pain a little until you can get help.

STINGER SAFETY

To stay safe from stingers when swimming, follow these simple rules:

• Only swim on beaches where jellyfish nets are used. Sea wasps are too big to swim through the mesh.

• Never swim alone. Stick to beaches that are patrolled by lifeguards. They will be able to help should you get into any trouble.

• Wear a "stinger suit" over your bathing suit. A full body suit is best as any exposed skin can get stung.

• Avoid the stinger season that runs from November to April, during the Australian summer. This is the time during which swimmers are at the greatest risk.

• Never touch jellyfish you find washed up on the beach. You can still receive a sting when they're dead.

HOW TO ROW ACROSS THE ATLANTIC

You are in La Gomera, an island in the Canary Islands, which are located in the Atlantic Ocean about 125 miles off the northwest coast of Africa. You are here to take part in the incredibly adventurous Atlantic Rowing Race, which takes place every two years. Ahead lies around 3,000 miles of open ocean between you and your destination, the tropical island of Antigua in the West Indies. If you are successful, the journey should take between 45 and 55 days.

The Atlantic is the world's second-largest ocean and rowing across is a real challenge. You'll be fine as long as you are ready to cope with high waves, strong winds, and curious sharks, not to mention blistered hands and a very sore behind.

ROW, ROW, ROW YOUR BOAT

To row across the Atlantic Ocean, you need to be physically and mentally prepared. Here are some tips for a trouble-free trip.

1. Pick your team. You can enter the race as a solo rower, in a pair, or in a team of four. If you decide to enter with a friend as a pair, pick your teammate carefully. You are going to be in that person's company all day, every day, for weeks on end.

2. Find a boat. Choose one that is made of fiberglass. Fiberglass is light, strong, and can be shaped for moving easily through choppy seas. The boat should have a small cabin, measuring about 2 yards long by a yard tall, in which you can rest when you're not rowing.

3. Get into training. You don't have to be an Olympic athlete to row across the Atlantic, but you will be pushing your body to its limits so you need to be very fit. Start training several months before the race. Begin by rowing short distances and then increase them to improve your stamina. Build your strength by lifting weights. Practice taking catnaps so you can sleep when you're not rowing. Between the two of you, you need to row for 24 hours a day, taking turns rowing for two hours followed by two hours' rest.

4. Plan your route well. The race route takes you across the Atlantic from east to west to take advantage of the most favorable winds and currents.

5. Pack your boat carefully. Pack heavy things low in the boat and make sure the weight is evenly spread. Make a list of where everything is and keep the things that you need the most handy.

ESSENTIAL SUPPLIES

• Freeze-dried food and high-energy snacks, such as peanuts, dried fruit, and PowerBars.

• A desalinator, used to convert salty sea water into fresh drinking water.

• A radio and a satellite telephone for communicating with your support team, other ships, and people at home.

• A GPS (Global Positioning System), sea charts, and a compass for navigating.

• A bilge pump, used for pumping out water when it comes over the side.

• A tool kit for repairing the boat, and spare oars.

• An emergency kit including a life raft, a first-aid kit, distress flares, a fire extinguisher, life jackets—all kept in easy reach in a waterproof bag in case you have to abandon your boat for the life raft.

HOW TO ROW A BOAT

Before you even think about rowing across the Atlantic, it is important to master the basics of rowing a boat. Take hold of the oars and follow these simple instructions as your first step toward your Atlantic adventure.

1. Sit with the bow—the pointy front end—of the boat behind you. Lean your body forward, stretching your arms out in front of you. Bend your knees as you put the blades of the oars into the water behind you, with the blades at right angles to the surface.

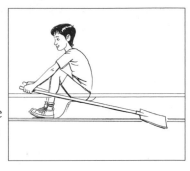

2. Lean back with your arms straight and then pull the oars by bringing your arms in toward you. Push with your legs as you do so.

3. When you have pulled the oars back as far as you can, raise them out of the water and twist your wrists so that the blades are now flat and parallel to the surface of the water.

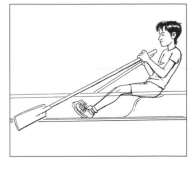

4. Lean your body forward and straighten your ams, then untwist your wrists to "square" the blades to get ready for your next stroke. Repeat steps 1–4.

HOW TO SING KARAOKE IN JAPAN

You hop on a plane and head off to Japan to visit your friends Yukiko and Kei. They are delighted to see you and have a special treat planned—a great night out. You are looking forward to entertainment, perhaps even a band, but when you arrive, you get a nasty surprise. *You* are the entertainment!

Your friends have brought you to a place where members of the audience take turns singing their favorite songs to wow the rest of the crowd. The Japanese name for this is karaoke, which means empty orchestra because there isn't an orchestra in sight. There is just a big video screen with the words to the songs scrolling across the bottom and enormous speakers blasting out the accompanying music. Resisting the urge to jump on the next plane home, you stick around. Yukiko and Kei give you some tips for making your turn at the microphone a memorable performance.

SINGING ALONG

• Try to remember it is just for fun. It doesn't matter if you aren't the greatest singer in the world. If you have a good time, so will the audience. Keep smiling and try to look confident, even if you're shaking with nerves.

• Choose a song you know very well and that shows off your singing abilities (or disguises your lack of them). Try to pick something catchy. That way, the audience is more likely to know it and join in.

• Watch the words on the screen very carefully even if you know the song.

• Give a performance. Don't just stand there, even if you're nervous. Let the emotions of the song show on your face and body movements, and dance a bit if it suits the song.

• At the end of your song, bow and graciously accept the applause.

Top tip: Before your next karaoke evening, practice your song at home. Use your hairbrush as a microphone to help you feel the part. Knowing the words better will help you to concentrate on your performance next time.

HOW TO FIND GRUB IN THE AUSTRALIAN OUTBACK

You're trekking through the outback—a vast area of wilderness, part desert, part scrubland, that stretches for thousands of miles in the middle of Australia. Apart from the odd kangaroo hopping by, there are very few living things around.

You're here to see if you can survive in one of the harshest places in the world. Your guide, Balun, is an Aborigine, which means he is descended from some of the first inhabitants of Australia. He has offered to show you how the Aborigines have been able to live off this land for thousands of years.

The outback, otherwise called the bush, might look like a wasteland, but there is a lot of food to be found if you know where to look. Aborigines used their incredible survival skills to hunt animals and gather nuts, seeds, berries, and fruits. Realizing you've left your lunchbox back at the camp, Balun offers to find you some "bush tucker" instead.

LOOKING FOR BUSH TUCKER

Bush tucker consists of anything you can find to eat in the bush—lizards, crocodiles, and even ants and grubs (the larvae of insects). Balun tells you that grubs called witchetty grubs are regarded as particular delicacies. They look like large maggots and are about as long and fat as your thumb. They are packed with vitamins and protein. They are the caterpillars of the cossid moth.

First you need to find a witchetty grub. Balun says that you need to look for witchetty bushes. These are very useful plants to the Aborigines, because they have edible seeds and sticky sap used by children as a type of chewing gum. More importantly, witchetty grubs bore into their roots. Tell-tale signs of this are small piles of sawdust around the base of a bush.

When you find a bush, Balun begins to dig around the roots with a sharp stick. He pulls out a root and shows you a hole in the side where he says a grub has burrowed. He breaks the root in two and pulls out a big juicy grub by its tail. Yummy!

GRUB'S UP

Traditionally, witchetty grubs are eaten raw and alive. Balun holds the grub by its head, pops it into his mouth, and bites off and eats the tail. He tells you that he prefers eating them raw as they taste slightly sweet with a creamy center, a bit like an egg. He finds another one and offers it to you. Your stomach heaves, but not wanting to be rude, you pop it in your mouth. You start chewing immediately to avoid feeling the grub wriggling around in your mouth. YUCK! You would rather have a cheese sandwich, but it isn't the worst thing you have ever tasted.

He sees you looking a bit squeamish and offers to cook up a delicious witchetty grub dip when you get back to his home. Follow the recipe below to make your own grubby dip.

GOURMET SHRIMPY SLIME

Balun uses real witchetty grubs in his recipe, but he says you could use shrimp instead. Remember to ALWAYS cook with an adult and ask permission to use the oven.

You will need:

• 5 oz witchetty grubs (or shrimp) • 1 tsp vegetable oil • pinch of salt • 1 roughly chopped spring onion • 1 cup low-fat sour cream • 3 oz reduced-fat cream cheese • toasted bread cut into triangles • carrot sticks for dipping.

1. Fry the grubs (or shrimp) in the oil until they are cooked through. Ask an adult to help you with this. Add the salt.

2. Put the grubs and the rest of the ingredients into a food processor and blend well. Ask an adult to help you with this.

3. Scrape your grubby dip out of the food processor and put it into a bowl.

4. Serve with toasted bread triangles and carrot sticks to dip, and garnish with whole grubs.

HOW TO RACE A HORSE IN MONGOLIA

Night has fallen, and the sky above you is full of twinkling stars. There's a crackling campfire and a sense of excitement in the air. You're on the flat, grassy plains of Mongolia with a family of herders who live in a large tent, called a *ger*. Everyone is very excited because tomorrow is the start of *Naadam*—the biggest and most important festival in the Mongolian year.

Naadam lasts for three days in the summer. It features singing and acrobatics, as well as archery competitions, wrestling, and horse racing—the three most popular Mongolian sports.

Your friend Ahduu and his son have been busy training their horses for months for the big race, but now his son has fallen ill and will be unable to ride. Ahduu has asked you to take his place in the race tomorrow. Feeling rather nervous, you eventually agree. Horses are a very important part of Mongolian life and you know how much Ahduu has been looking forward to the race. It's an honor to be asked, but you also know how tough and grueling these cross-country races can be, both for the horses and the jockeys. You'd better get some sleep so you're rested and in good shape for tomorrow.

IT'S RACE DAY

As day dawns, Ahduu's wife pours him a bowl of *airag*—the sweet, fermented horse milk that's a popular drink around here. She wishes you luck, as Ahduu takes you to meet your horse, and walks with you to the nearby venue for the race.

Your horse's name is Jiinst. He is small and stocky like all Mongolian horses. They're famous for their strength and stamina, and luckily for you, they can run for hours without getting tired. Today, Jiinst's tail has been braided and his mane is tied up in a bright ribbon for the race. As you walk, Ahduu sings softly to the horse for luck. He tells you that these songs, which ask the horses to ride fast and be strong, have been around for centuries.

When you reach the starting line, you mount Jiinst and promise Ahduu that you'll do your best. Looking around, you can see many other children on horses getting ready for the races—some of them are as young as five years old. There are around a thousand horses that have been picked to take part, and the noise of whinnying and stamping of hooves fills the air.

AND THEY'RE OFF . . .

1. You wait for your race to be announced. There are six races to choose from, depending on a horse's age. The length of each race varies accordingly. Jiinst is only two years old, so Ahduu has entered you in the 9½-mile race. Older horses run twice that distance.

2. Before the race, you ride three times around the Mongolian flag while the audience sings traditional songs. Then Ahduu leads you between rows of cheering spectators to the start line. The signal is given, a cloud of dust flies up, and away you go.

3. You and Jiinst race across the dusty plains. You shout, "*Googto!*" to urge him on. There's no track or course to follow, so you just try to keep up with the horse in front. It's very tough going, and, once or twice, you nearly fall off. Luckily, it's the horse, not the rider, that wins the race and the horses are trained to keep running even if they lose their jockeys.

4. You reach the halfway marker and turn back, heading for home. Just as you reach the finish, you overtake the leading horse and cross the line first. To Ahduu's delight, you've won! The race has taken you three hours and both you and Jiinst are exhausted.

5. You lead Jiinst up to collect his prize. He receives a gold medal and has a poem written in his honor. (There are silver and bronze medals for the horses finishing second and third.) Ahduu steps up to collect his prize money. Crowds of people follow you, touching Jiinst's flanks and then wiping their faces. Ahduu explains that the horse's sweat will bring good luck for the rest of the year. He recommends you wipe some on your face.

The race is over, but *Naadam* is far from finished. You and Ahduu head to the stadium to watch the wrestling contests, and you look forward to enjoying all of the festivities before getting some well-earned rest.

HOW TO AVOID ALTITUDE SICKNESS ON MOUNT KILIMANJARO

Surrounded by thick, tropical rain forest, you can feel a trickle of sweat slowly sliding down your back underneath your backpack. You are 1 mile up Mount Kilimanjaro, Africa's highest mountain, in Tanzania, East Africa.

Mount Kilimanjaro is one of the "Seven Summits"—the highest points on each of the seven continents in the world—and climbing all seven is one of the greatest challenges in mountaineering.

Kilimanjaro's Uhuru Peak is the first peak on your to-do list, but it is going to be tough. At an incredible 3.6 miles high, it towers above the surrounding plains. While there are several routes to choose from, you are taking the Machame Route up the mountain, which is famous for its beautiful views. Your climb begins in the rain forests and moorlands, then crosses a river, before reaching the rockier slopes near the top. Climbing the mountain involves walking for up to seven hours a day, covering a distance of between 6 and 12 miles. Each evening, you stop to camp. The porters that are accompanying you set up tents and cooking gear. After breakfast each morning, you set off again up the mountain.

ALTITUDE SICKNESS STRIKES

Less than halfway up the mountain, you start feeling dizzy, and your head begins to ache. With every step, you feel worse, so you tell your guide. He tells you that you are suffering from altitude sickness. Altitude sickness is the most common health problem climbers face when climbing more than 1.5 miles above sea level. It happens when your body reacts to the thinner air at high altitudes. Thinner air makes it difficult for your lungs to get enough oxygen into your body.

Your symptoms are relatively mild and your guide advises you to slow your pace up the mountain. It might take a couple of days for you to feel completely better, but slowing your pace will allow your body to get used to the thinner air more gradually.

AVOIDING ALTITUDE SICKNESS

Your guide explains it is impossible to prevent altitude sickness, but you can take some precautions:

• Don't go too high too fast. Keep at a slow, steady pace from day one. If you begin to feel ill, slow down until you feel better.

• If you feel worse—for example, you have a headache that doesn't go away—descending the mountain by as little as 500 yards can help. Stay there until the symptoms pass. Then test yourself by trying to walk in a straight line. If you can't, you need to go further down the mountain.

• If you are short of breath—even when you're sitting down—and you can't walk, your symptoms count as severe. You must descend the mountain immediately.

• If you don't feel well enough to walk, get into a Gamow bag. A Gamow bag is a nylon tube with a pump that is inflated once a climber is inside. This creates conditions more similar to those at a lower altitude and relieves the pressure on your lungs, helping them to work properly again. After an hour or two, you should feel well enough to walk down the mountain on your own.

WARNING

Altitude sickness can be very dangerous. In the worst cases, fluid can build up in your lungs and brain, which can kill you if you don't get urgent medical treatment.

SUMMIT SUCCESS

As soon as you start to feel better, you continue your trek up the mountain. On day six, you try for the summit. You have to get up at midnight and begin the steepest and most grueling part of the climb. You climb for around four hours, then stop for a short rest. After walking through snow for another two hours, you reach Uhuru Peak at sunrise. The views are definitely worth it. Well done, you've climbed one of the seven summits...only six more to go before you become a mountaineering hero!

HOW TO TAKE PART IN THE HIGHLAND GAMES

The sound of bagpipes means you must be in Scotland, where you have arrived for the annual Highland Games. The Games are held all over the country, and are especially popular in the Highlands (the rugged, mountainous region in the north). You decide to give the bagpipe playing and dancing competitions a miss, and enter one of the most famous events—tossing the caber.

TOSSING THE CABER

A caber is the trunk of a pine tree. It measures about 20 feet long and weighs more than an average adult man. A Games' official sets the caber on its end, with its thickest end in the air.

1. Bend toward the caber and allow it to rest against your right shoulder. Clasp your arms around it, interlocking your fingers. Bend your knees and slide your hands down the caber toward the base. Cup the palms of your hands underneath the base. Straighten your legs and lift the caber off the ground, still supporting it with your shoulder.

2. With your hands cupped around the end of the caber, run forward, slowly at first, and then try to build up some speed.

3. To toss the caber into the air, stop running and quickly push the caber up and away from you so that it flips over and lands on its thicker end.

If you haven't tossed it very far, it doesn't matter. The winning thrower is not the one who tosses the caber the farthest, but the one whose caber lands in the straightest line parallel to the direction of the runner's approach.

Your caber wobbles on its end, then falls forward almost perfectly parallel to the direction of your approach. Now, you have to wait to see if any of the other competitors can beat your throw.

Top tip: If a caber is hard to come by and rather too large, practice your technique with a broom handle. Be careful not to harm yourself and others while learning.

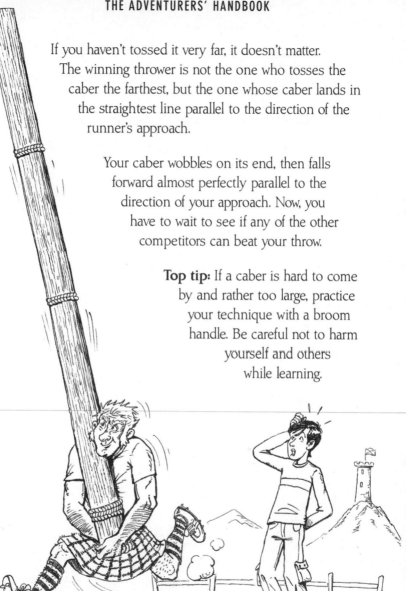

HOLD YOUR OWN HIGHLAND GAMES

Besides the famous caber toss, there are lots of other events at the Highland Games that you can practice at home for your next visit. Why not hold your own Highland Games to hone your skills?

TUG-OF-WAR

You will need:
• two teams of at least two players • a judge
• a length of rope or an old bedsheet • a stopwatch • duct tape

1. Find the middle of the rope by folding it in half. Mark the midpoint by wrapping a piece of duct tape around it.

2. Mark the ground using duct tape to show where the midpoint of the rope should be at the start of the competition. Lay out the rope so that its midpoint lies on the taped line.

3. The two teams then line up opposite one another, next to their end of the rope.

4. The judge calls "Pick up the rope," and each player picks up the rope and holds on to it with both hands—pulling it tight but not attempting to tug. The judge must make sure the midpoint marker is directly over the start line on the ground before the game can begin.

5. When the judge is happy with the starting position, he calls "Pull!" and starts the stopwatch. Each team has to start pulling on the rope as hard as they can. Players should keep their arms almost straight and bend their knees, digging into the ground with their heels. Each team needs to pull together.

6. After two minutes, the judge shouts "Stop!" and all the players have to freeze. The winning team is the team who has managed to pull the midpoint of the rope farthest across the start line. The judge's decision is final.

7. The teams change ends for the next round. The team that wins the best of three rounds is the final winner.

WELLY WANGING

Try welly wanging, played in many junior Highland events. (Welly is slang for a rubber boot. Wanging means to throw.)

You will need:

• duct tape • 3 Wellington or other rubber boots • an open space

1. First decide where your start line will be. This will be the point from which you will throw the boot. Make sure there is a big, open space beyond it so that you don't damage anything. Mark the start line with tape.

2. Decide who will go first. That person picks up a welly and holds it at the open end.

3. The idea of the game is to throw the boot as far as possible from the start line. Stand sideways to the starting line with your welly in your hand. Swing the welly forward and back again a few times to gather momentum. When you're ready, launch the welly as far as you can into the throwing arena. Experiment with different throwing techniques to see which one works the best. Each player gets three throws and the best of the three is marked with tape. (You must mark the spot where the welly first lands, not the place it comes to rest after bouncing.)

4. The player who throws the welly that lands the farthest from the start line is the winner.

If the winner of this game was also in the winning team of the Tug-of-War, they are the champion of the Games.

HOW TO HANG TEN IN HAWAII

An almighty wave comes crashing down over your head, dragging you down, deep under water. You've just "wiped out"—which means you have been knocked off your surfboard into the sea. Coughing and spluttering, you drag yourself back up to the shore to get some much-needed lessons.

You've picked Hawaii to learn to surf because it has some of the best surfing spots in the world—the waves off the North Shore can reach as high as 20 feet in the winter. Hawaii is made up of a group of islands in the Pacific Ocean. The islands are actually the tops of vast volcanoes that rise up from the seabed. Eruptions of hot lava have cooled, causing ridges to form along the bottom of the seabed. When water is pushed over the ridges by the tides, gigantic waves are formed.

SURF'S UP—LESSONS IN CATCHING WAVES

Farther up the beach you spot a surfing instructor teaching a group of tourists how to catch a wave. You quickly ask to join the class, board in tow.

Before you get into the sea, the instructor shows you something called the pop-up—this is how you jump from lying on your board to standing up.

THE PERFECT POP-UP

1. Lie facedown on your board. Push your palms down flat on the middle of the board. Use your arms to push yourself up. Then, in one fluid motion, jump your feet up and under your body so that your knees are beneath your chest and you are standing on your board.

2. As you land, place your back foot (this is your left foot if you are right-handed) toward the tail or end of your board and your right foot just above the middle. You should end up with your knees bent and your chin above the center of the board.

The pop-up is quite tricky to master so you practice it on the beach until you get it right.

HITTING THE SURF

Now you have perfected the pop-up, it is time to get your face out of the sand and into the surf.

• Get strapped in. Attach the leash (safety strap) on your board around the ankle of your back leg. If you fall off in the water, you'll be able to keep hold of your board. Drifting boards can be very dangerous to other surfers and swimmers.

• Paddle out. Walk into the sea, holding your board at arm's length, with a hand on either side so the waves don't knock it back into your face. When the water is about waist high, lie facedown on your board. Keep your weight centered on the middle of the board and try not to lean back, otherwise the nose (front) of your board may flip up and knock you off. Start paddling, scooping water with your hands until you are beyond the point where the waves are breaking.

• Duck-dive. If you meet a large wave as you're paddling out, go under not over it. This is called duck-diving. To do this, shift your weight forward to lower the nose of your board so it goes under the water. Your board is made of foam and fiberglass. It is very buoyant and will quickly float you safely back to the surface once you're past the wave.

• Catch a wave. Look at the waves coming toward you and pick one that looks big enough to carry you along. Turn the nose of your board to face the beach and start paddling as fast as you can.

• Pop-up. As you feel the wave beginning to carry you along, stop paddling and try to pop-up, just as you did on the beach.

• Ride the wave. To stop yourself falling off, stretch your arms out to the side, keeping your legs slightly bent at the knees at all times. Keep your board at an angle to the wave, and ride to the shore. Keep looking in the direction you want to go and the board will follow. Lean your weight from side to side to change direction.

Top tip: Try to focus your eyes on the part of the wave that you want to surf. This helps to keep you balanced on the board and avoid any spectacular wipeouts.

HOW TO REMOVE A LEECH IN MADAGASCAR

You arrive on Madagascar, a large island off the east coast of Africa. The island is famous for its fascinating wildlife, over 80 percent of which is found nowhere else on Earth. The best-known animals on the island are the lemurs, a type of primate—like monkeys and gorillas. The most famous are the ring-tailed lemurs.

You are here on a mission to spot the endangered indri, the largest type of lemur, which lives in the rain forest on the east coast of Madagascar. Today, its numbers have seriously dwindled

because its habitat is being destroyed for timber and to make space for farmland.

Your local guide, Jaona, leads you to a part of the rain forest where he has seen indris before. But despite their striking black and white coloring, they prove very hard to find. You're about to give up, when you hear an eerie wailing—it is the indri's distinctive cry. You reach down to get your binoculars out of your bag—and notice a fat, shiny leech feasting on your leg.

BLOODSUCKERS

Leeches are worm-like creatures, flattened at one end. They like to live in warm, damp places, so rain forests are an ideal home. After heavy rain, they hang from leaves and branches, waiting for their next meal—animal or human—to walk by. Then they drop down, stick on with their strong suckers at either end, and start to suck blood. When one lands on you, you probably won't feel a thing because the leech produces an anesthetic that numbs your skin.

The good news is leech bites don't hurt, but the wound may bleed profusely. This is because the leech also produces a chemical called an anti-coagulant that stops your blood from clotting and forming a scab. The bad news is, because the rain forest is full of leeches, the slimy suckers are almost impossible to avoid.

LEECH REMOVAL TIPS

If a leech attaches itself to you, don't panic. Leeches usually drop off when they've finished gorging on your blood. They can drink ten times their own weight in blood in a single meal. Unfortunately, leeches can carry some viruses, so you will probably want to get rid of them before that.

1. To do this, slide your fingernail under the sucker near the leech's mouth (this is the thin end), and scrape it off. Do the same to the sucker at the rear. Be careful not to let the leech reattach itself. Then flick it away.

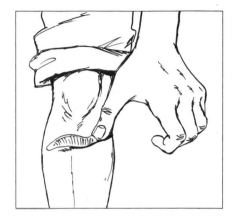

2. Keep any leech wounds clean. In the rainforest climate, wounds can quickly become infected. They will bleed until the anti-coagulant has washed away, and they will be itchy while they heal, but don't be tempted to scratch them.

Avoid leeches by wearing long pants instead of shorts, and a long-sleeved shirt to leave less of your skin exposed to leeches. Tuck your pants into your socks or wear leech socks (special socks that go over your socks but inside your shoes). They come up to just above your calves and hungry leeches can't bite through them.

Top tip: Never try to just pull or burn a leech off while it's feeding. Bits of its jaws may get left in your skin, causing an infection. Burning off a leech can cause it to regurgitate (throw up) its last meal into you, which can also lead to infection.

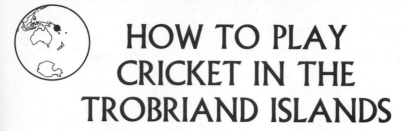

HOW TO PLAY CRICKET IN THE TROBRIAND ISLANDS

You travel to the Trobriand Islands, a small group of coral islands in the Pacific Ocean, off the east coast of New Guinea. You land on the main island of Kiriwina, where most of the 15,000 islanders live. But the island's sandy beaches and lush rain forests will have to wait. Unlikely as it sounds, you are here to play cricket–the islanders' favorite game.

Your guide, Moyabwau, explains that the islanders have been playing cricket since the beginning of the 20th century. Instead of going to war against rival villages, islanders began challenging each other to cricket matches. But if you're expecting players dressed all in white, hushed crowds, and polite applause, you are in for a surprise. Cricket Trobriand-style is not like cricket anywhere else in the world.

RULES OF THE GAME

Just in case, you have brought your cricket whites, but Moyabwau explains that you won't need them. For Trobriand cricket, you dress like a warrior with war paint on your face and body, armbands, and feathers in your hair. Apart from that, you only wear a loincloth–a piece of cloth wrapped around your bottom like a large diaper. You won't need your sneakers either; Trobrianders play cricket barefoot.

As in traditional cricket, you play with a bat and a ball, but the bat is more like a baseball bat than a cricket bat. It is painted black and white. Before the match, you take the bats and balls to a local magician who puts a good luck spell on them. He also calls on the spirits to send good weather for the match.

You go and join your team. Traditionally, cricket is played between two teams of eleven players, but in Trobriand cricket, teams include all the men from the competing villages and may have as many as 50 to 60 players. All that matters is that the number of players on each team is the same.

The teams take to the field. Each chants and performs a war dance, composed especially for the match and practiced for hours beforehand. Meanwhile, the crowd whoops and cheers, and some people blow into conch shells to urge on their team.

Cricket is a complicated game. To learn more about it, visit the
International Cricket Council Web site at http://icc-cricket.yahoo.net.

Under Trobriand rules, the visiting team bats first. As you are a
guest, they let you go first. You and Moyabwau take your places in
front of the wickets at either end.

You can only score a run if you hit the ball. If you hit it really hard
and it goes above the highest coconut trees, you score a *nosibol,*
which is six runs. The chief of another village is appointed as
scorekeeper. He keeps score by cutting notches into a palm frond.

Trobriand bowlers (pitchers) bowl underhand. The bowler runs
forward and bowls the ball. You concentrate on the ball and swing
your bat—*thwack!* The ball soars into the air. You start to run, but
hope the ball will sail above the trees. As it goes higher you slow
down—surely you have done enough to score a *nosibol?* All of a

sudden, you hear a cheer from behind you. You think you've done it, but you haven't—a member of the fielding team has caught it and is leaping into the air, shouting. You are out.

Outs are decided by the umpire, who is from the batting team. As in traditional cricket rules, the batter is out if the ball hits the stumps (like a goalpost) or is caught by one of the fielding team. Every time a batter is out, the fielding team celebrates with a war dance in the middle of the playing field. As they take to the middle, you join the spectators.

An inning lasts until all of the batters have been declared out, and all the dances have been performed. This can take several hours. Then the teams change sides. In a day, each team usually has two innings, so a match can last for 8 hours or more.

The home team is always declared the winner, no matter what the score is. The two teams exchange gifts of yams, and the home team puts on a celebratory feast. There are no trophies for the winners, but gifts of yams are presented to the best bowler, batter, captain, and scorekeeper.

Top tip: The most important matches of the year take place at the time of the annual yam harvest. Yams are the most important crop on the Trobriand Islands and the islanders' staple food.

HOW TO SURVIVE THE "BIG ONE" IN SAN FRANCISCO

Suddenly, you feel the earth moving very slightly beneath your feet. The earth shakes again and you worry this might be the sign of something bigger to come. You've come to the city of San Francisco, California, to study earthquakes and it looks like you've arrived at the right time—or is it the wrong time?

Luckily for you, this is only a slight tremor and it passes quickly. Unluckily for the residents of San Francisco, however, the city sits almost on top of a massive 620-mile-long fault, called the

San Andreas Fault. A fault is a place where two of the moving plates (sections) of the Earth's crust meet. When the two plates catch as they move against each other, they bend and squash the rocks at the edges. As the pressure increases, the plates suddenly slip, and then catch again. This sudden jerking sends shock waves shooting through the Earth, causing an earthquake.

Feeling a little shaken, you head straight to the lab where Angela, an earthquake specialist, is expecting you to begin your work.

MEASURING EARTHQUAKES

Relieved to see you are OK, Angela explains that these tremors are not uncommon; tiny shakes hit the region all the time. San Francisco has known much bigger ones in its past. In 1906 and 1989, movements along the San Andreas Fault caused two gigantic earthquakes, destroying homes and buildings, killing and injuring many people. She explains that earthquakes are measured using something called the Richter Scale. Developed in 1935, it rates an earthquake's magnitude (the amount of energy it releases). On the scale below, each level up is ten times the magnitude of the last. The 1906 San Francisco quake is estimated to have measured 7.8 on the Richter Scale; the 1989 quake measured 6.9.

EARTHQUAKE SURVIVAL

Measurement	Effect
1.0–2.9	Generally not felt, but recorded by seismographs.
3.0–3.9	Felt by some people, but rarely causes any damage.
4.0–4.9	Felt by everyone, breaks household objects.
5.0–5.9	Some damage to poorly constructed buildings.
6.0–6.9	Fairly destructive in populated areas.
7.0–7.9	Major earthquake. Serious damage over large area.
8.0 or above	Great earthquake. Major damage over huge area.

Experts think there's at least a 60 percent chance of the next "Big One" striking by 2030, and the city needs to make sure it has lots of warning. Angela hands you a seismograph (a piece of equipment that measures the slightest movements in the ground), and sends you off to record any rumblings going on. Before you disappear, she gives you some essential earthquake survival advice.

• If you are indoors, stay there. Children in California practice the drill DROP, COVER, AND HOLD ON. This means: DROP down near the floor, take COVER under a heavy piece of furniture such as a table or desk, and HOLD ON.

• Protect your head with a cushion or pillow. Steer clear of windows and doors.

• Stay away from the stairs—you might fall down them. Never try to use an elevator—you could be trapped if the power fails.

• If you are outdoors, find an open space away from buildings, chimneys, trees, and power lines, because these could fall on top of you. Crouch down on the ground while the quake lasts. If you are on a city street, find a strong archway or a doorframe to shelter in.

• If you are in a car, get the driver to slow down and drive to an open space. Don't stop near bridges or underpasses in case they collapse. Stay in the car until the shaking stops. Then drive on very slowly, because the roads may have been damaged by the quake.

AFTER AN EARTHQUAKE

• Be prepared for further earthquakes called aftershocks. After the 1989 earthquake in San Francisco, some 30,000 aftershocks followed.

• Check yourself and others for injuries. Only use the telephone to call for help if it's an emergency—you could stop vital calls from getting through.

• Check for other hazards, such as fires and gas leaks. Turn off the gas and electricity if you suspect anything is wrong. Don't drink water from the tap or use the toilet because the pipes may be cracked or damaged.

• Listen to the radio for information and instructions.

HOW TO RIDE THE RAPIDS IN THE ROCKIES

Along with seven intrepid friends and your rafting guide, Alanna, you are exploring a stretch of the upper Colorado River. The Colorado River rises in the Rocky Mountains of Colorado, and flows for more than 1,400 miles to Northwest Mexico. It runs through some of the most spectacular scenery on the planet, including the Grand Canyon in Arizona, which is considered one of the greatest wonders of the natural world.

Alanna explains that the water in this section of the river is moving quite fast at the moment due to water from melted snow draining down from the mountains after the spring thaw.

Rapids are classified to warn people how fast the water is moving. The class of rapids you will be attempting ranges from I to IV, but in one or two places, you might encounter level V rapids, so it's vital to be prepared and keep your wits about you.

USA RAPIDS CLASSES

Class	Conditions
I	Mostly calm water with few rough areas. Little steering needed.
II	Some rough water and rocks. Steering around rocks necessary.
III	Some white water and fast currents, but no real danger.
IV	Very difficult. White water, fast currents, and rocks. Skilled steering required.
V	Extremely difficult. White water, large rocks, strong currents, large drops, and holes. Requires advanced steering.
VI	So dangerous that they are almost impossible to ride safely. Very likely to result in serious injury or even death.

Most rivers don't fit neatly into one category. Classes I and II are suitable for complete beginners. Classes III and IV are best for confident beginners and intermediate paddlers. Classes V and VI are for experts only. So get ready for a challenge.

BEFORE YOU START

• The correct safety equipment is essential for white-water rafting. You'll need to wear a close-fitting life jacket in case you end up going for an unexpected swim. The jacket will stop your back and shoulders from getting bumped and bruised— and it will keep you afloat. You won't be going anywhere without a crash helmet either, so strap it on securely to protect your head.

• Scout ahead for danger by walking along the bank before you set foot in the raft. Check for sudden changes in the direction of the current and for hazards, such as rocks and fallen trees.

GET RAFTING

• White-water rafts are large, inflatable boats made from very strong rubber. There is room for eight paddlers and Alanna in this raft. Alanna is in charge of steering the raft, and sits at the back, using a paddle as a rudder. The rest of you half sit, half kneel on the edges of the raft as she makes sure the crew's weight is spread out evenly and that the boat is well balanced.

• Alanna explains all the instructions she will be using and shows you the basics of paddling. She lets you practice on a stretch of calm water before you reach the rapids. Hold the handle of the paddle in both hands and move the blade through the water with long, smooth strokes. Practice paddling forward and backward (back paddling slows the raft down).

ON THE MOVE

Once you start paddling for real, Alanna shouts instructions, pointing out any rocks or fallen trees. If you get stuck on a rock, there are a couple of things you can do. You could get out of the raft and give it a push, keeping a secure hold on the side of the raft, but the rocks are slippery and you might lose your footing

and go under. Alternatively, you and your fellow paddlers can work out the location of the rock and shift your weight to the other end of the raft. Then, you should be able to use your paddles to push off and away from the rock.

Although you have an experienced guide to show you the ropes, you should still look ahead for safe places to rest. These are called eddies, and are formed where the water circles behind a rock or log. They allow you time to catch your breath before the next leg of your journey.

WILD RIDE

You quickly come to grips with paddling and keeping your balance, and just in time. Just around the next bend in the river is your first serious drop. The water plunges down 10 feet and suddenly, your heart is in your mouth as you get some serious air time. Lean back and enjoy the ride. Keep a good grip on your paddle for when you land, and start paddling immediately to pull the raft away from the white water.

Top tip: If you fall out of the raft, try to keep hold of the side—if you can't, then try to swim back to it, but don't let go of your paddle. Your crew will need to grab hold of it to pull you back on board. Alternatively, lie on your back, with your feet pointing downstream and float toward the shore. Use your arms to steer. Your life jacket will stop you from sinking and Alanna is trained in white-water rescue. If there is a strong current, don't try to stand up. You will be knocked over by the water and if it's rocky, you risk getting your foot caught and being dragged under.

HOW TO AVOID HIPPOS ON THE ZAMBEZI

You're standing on the bank of the Zambezi River, the fourth longest river in Africa. It's early in the morning, and you are off to do some bird-watching. You've picked the ideal spot. The river is home to hundreds of species of birds, including pelicans and storks.

Armed with your binoculars, you set off in your canoe. Before you and your companion, David, have paddled very far, an enormous black shape looms in the water ahead. You're on a stretch of the river frequented by elephants, buffaloes, zebras, giraffes, crocodiles, and hippos. At first, you think the bulky shape is a crocodile, but it's more dangerous than that—it's a hippopotamus.

HIPPO ALERT

David tells you that despite their chilled-out appearance, hippos can be very aggressive. They can be killers—not simply because of their enormous bulk (a male can weigh almost 4 tons), but because males have huge canine teeth up to 2 feet long, which they use as lethal weapons for fighting off rivals.

You are unlikely to survive an attack by a hippo, so your best strategy is to steer your canoe clear of it.

• Stick to shallow water—leave the deeper water to the hippos.

• If you have to cross a deep channel, bang on the side of your canoe or slap the water with your paddle to warn the hippo you're approaching.

• A hippo may attack boats and canoes if they come too close. The trouble is that you might not notice a hippo charging until

it has hit you full-on. A hippo can hold its breath under water for five minutes while it runs along the bottom of the river. Look out for a V-shaped wave in the water that could signal an angry hippo below the surface.

• If you meet a hippo on dry land, don't get between it and the river. It will feel threatened and may attack.

• Don't even think about trying to outrun a hippo. They can charge along at speeds of up to 30 miles an hour, which is much faster than you can run, but they can't climb trees. Get to a tree and climb up it fast.

Top tip: If you spot a family of mother hippos and their babies, make a detour and avoid them at all costs. Female hippos are fiercely protective of their young and will attack if they feel they are in danger.

HOW TO DO TAI CHI IN CHINA

You arrive in Shanghai, China. It is an amazing city, full of ancient palaces and temples, huge skyscrapers, and busy traffic. However, you are not here to take in the sights. You're here to learn how to do tai chi, an ancient Chinese martial art, today often practiced as a form of exercise. You are lucky because your teacher is Wan Cheng, one of the greatest tai chi masters.

Tai chi is based on different sets of postures, or exercises, performed with slow, flowing movements. It was first practiced in China almost two thousand years ago. Wan Cheng tells you that he believes that the body is filled with energy called chi. If the flow of energy gets blocked, it can cause injuries and illnesses. By doing tai chi, you can smooth the flow of chi through your body, and improve your health and well-being. People also find tai chi helps to reduce stress and makes them stronger and more flexible.

To practice tai chi, you should wear something comfortable and loose so you can move and stretch easily. Tai chi is usually performed in bare feet and it is best to do your exercises outside or in a room that has plenty of space.

Before you begin, Wan Cheng tells you that breathing properly is essential while you are doing the exercises. First, relax and clear your mind of any thoughts and distractions. Breathe deeply and evenly through your nose. You may need to practice this until it comes naturally. When you breathe in, your diaphragm (the flat sheet of muscle under your lungs) moves outward and downward to allow your lungs to take in fresh air. When you breathe out, your diaphragm contracts (squeezes) inward and upward to push stale air out. Wan Cheng reminds you that correct breathing leads to a calm state of mind.

Now you are ready to perform your first exercise. Wan Cheng tells you it is called the "Horse riding Stance" because it looks as if you are riding a horse. You must return to this posture when you are moving from one exercise to the next so it is important to get it right. Wan Cheng demonstrates the movements while you copy what he is doing.

HORSE RIDING STANCE

1. Stand with your feet a little wider than shoulder-width apart. Your feet should be parallel to each other and directly under your knees.

2. Bend your knees slightly, then sink down into a squatting or sitting position. By doing this, your center of gravity should be perfectly balanced down the middle of your body.

3. Keeping your back straight and head held high, lift your arms out in front of you, palms facing inward. Keep your elbows relaxed and slightly bent as if you are holding a horse's reins, or hugging a tree.

4. Take a deep breath, then breathe out again to relax your body and release any tension. Hold this stance for as long as possible. To begin with, you may only be able to manage a minute or two before your legs start feeling tired. As your leg muscles get stronger, you will be able to hold the stance for longer.

Top tip: Don't let your shoulders hunch up, but try to keep your whole body relaxed. Remember that each posture in tai chi should be performed in one long, flowing movement.

HOW TO TAKE PART IN THE CARNIVAL IN RIO

You've arrived in the bustling city of Rio de Janeiro in Brazil. It's February and it's carnival time. This is when the city puts on a dazzling four-day show of music, dancing, and merrymaking, before the fasting of Lent begins.

You are here to take part in the spectacular samba parade, the showstopping highlight of carnival week which takes place over two nights on Sunday and Monday. During the parade, thousands of elaborately dressed dancers, samba drummers, and fabulous floats from the city's rival samba schools compete for the sought-after title of carnival champions.

You'll be joining the Grande Rio School, one of the best in the city. The other members of the school have spent months designing the floats and elaborate costumes for their dance down the Sambadrome—the long avenue on which the parade takes place.

This year, the Grande Rio School has chosen the rain forest as its theme, and as parade time draws near, you see more and more of your fellow paraders emerging in stunning costumes. Lots of them look like exotic rain forest birds, wearing feathers, sequins, pompoms, and glitter, with jewel-encrusted wings in red, green, and white.

You've been practicing your samba steps, but before you can join the parade along the Sambadrome, you'll need to look the part.

MAKE A BIRD OF PARADISE HEADDRESS

You will need:

• a piece of string • a ruler • heavy paper or posterboard • scissors • glue • Scotch tape • colored craft feathers of different sizes • felt-tip pens • glitter • sequins

1. Measure around your head using a piece of string. To do this, hold your string at one end against your forehead, 1 inch above your eyebrows, and wrap the rest of it around your head until the length of the string touches the end. Keep hold of the string at the point where it meets the loose end and measure from that point to the end using your ruler. Make a note of the length of your string.

2. Lay the paper down lengthways in front of you. Measure from the left edge of the paper the length you noted down and mark it clearly.

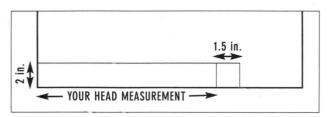

3. Measure and mark 2 in. up from the edge of the card nearest you. Use this mark to draw a rectangle 2 in. by the length of your string. Add an extra 1.5 in. to the right of your rectangle. This will be used to fasten your headdress. Cut it out.

4. Turn your strip of card over and use felt-tip pens to draw on the brightest, craziest designs that you can. When all the white of your card is covered, dot your strip with blobs of glue and sprinkle it with glitter and sequins. Leave it to dry.

5. Once the glue is dry, turn the card over and arrange your feathers. One large feather in the center, with several other feathers fanning out on either side of it, looks particularly impressive. Secure using tape.

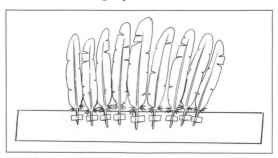

6. Bend the card into a circle, so that the ends overlap by 1.5 in., and tape the ends together securely. You should now have a colorful carnival headdress that fits on your head snugly.

7. Pop it on your head and you're ready to dance the night away in Rio's carnival.

HOW TO HERD REINDEER WITH THE SAMI

You hear the *swoosh* of a snowmobile and a figure dressed in a blue-and-red coat pulls up next to you. It is Nils, your Sami guide. You have traveled to the far north of Norway to help Nils and his family herd their reindeer. The Sami people are a community of reindeer herders that live across Northern Scandinavia and Russia. Over a cup of strong Sami coffee, Nils tells you about what life is like being a Sami reindeer herder.

REINDEER KNOW-HOW

During the year, the reindeer move from place to place looking for fresh pastures of grass and lichen. The herders follow behind on snowmobiles and skis, covering hundreds of miles a year.

On the move, Nils and his family live in a tent called a *lavvu*, which can be packed up each morning and loaded on to a sled.

Reindeer are well suited to the harsh conditions they live in. They have thick coats made up of hollow hairs to trap warm air close to their bodies. Their hooves are broad and slightly curved for moving easily over the snow and digging plants buried beneath it.

FOLLOWING THE HERD

For centuries, the Sami have relied on reindeer for transportation, meat, milk, and hides for clothing and to trade. They use every part of a reindeer, including the tendons and sinews for sewing thread. You have joined Nils and his family as the reindeer are heading toward the coast where there is plenty of grass to eat.

When you reach the coast, the reindeer wander off to graze. You can relax a little, but you do have to jump up occasionally to rescue a reindeer that is about to fall from a cliff, or one that is wandering too far from the herd. The Sami do this using lassos just like cowboys in the U.S. They throw the rope so that it loops around a reindeer's antlers. The rope has a special knot called a honda knot that tightens around the antlers when the rope is pulled. Nils shows you how to tie a rope so that you can use it as a lasso.

The reindeer start to move inland in search of more grass and fungi to eat. You spend a lot of your time on your snowmobile, looking for missing reindeer and keeping the herd together. Nils's animals have his distinctive mark on their ears, making them easy to identify. You round up any stragglers with your lasso.

HOW TO TIE A LASSO

1. Tie an ordinary knot in the end of your rope. This will act as a stopper to prevent your lasso from unraveling.

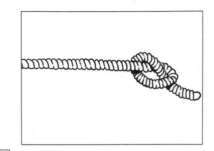

2. Make a loop in your rope, as shown here.

3. Make a bend in your rope on the knot side of the loop you have just made. Feed this bend through the loop and pull the loop tight around it.

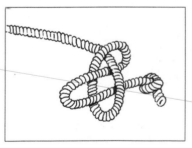

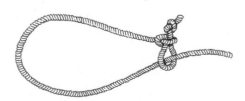

4. Feed the loose end of your rope through the bend with the loop tightened around it. This is your lasso.

HOW TO THROW A LASSO

Now you have mastered tying your lasso, it is time to learn how to use it. Nils says it is best to practice throwing your lasso around a tree stump because it doesn't move.

He asks you to stand about 5 yards back from a suitable-looking stump and demonstrates how best to throw.

1. Take the loop in your right hand and hold it about 4 inches from the knot. Loosen the loop until it is about a yard across.

2. The rope should be coiled so that it will unfurl freely when the loop is thrown. Hold the coil in your left hand.

3. Spin the lasso over your head by tracing a clockwise circle in the air with your wrist.

4. When you are ready to throw, step forward quickly in the direction of the stump. Release the spinning rope by bringing your arm forward and down to shoulder level as you let go of it.

5. If you have got your throw right, the loop should fly toward your target and encircle it. If this happens, pull on the end of the rope in your left hand to tighten the loop.

6. When the loop is tightened, hang on tight. The tree stump might not be going anywhere, but a reindeer is likely to try and run off, taking your rope (and you) with it.

HOW TO CROSS
THE BERING STRAIT

You are standing on one of the wildest spots in the world—the shores of Cape Prince of Wales in Alaska. This is the westernmost point in North America. Only 53 miles farther west lies Cape Dezhnev, in northeastern Russia. The wind is howling around your ears and it is awfully cold. You are here to take part in an amazing journey. You are hoping to cross the Bering Strait.

The Bering Strait is a narrow channel of water separating Asia and North America. It connects the Chukchi Sea (part of the Arctic Ocean in the north) to the Bering Sea (part of the Pacific Ocean in the south). Directly in the middle lie the Diomede Islands, where you can stop to rest on your crossing. Although it looks short on a map, crossing the Bering Strait is highly dangerous. For starters, the water is choppy and treacherous and, in the winter, it's covered in ice that is constantly moving and breaking off. Despite the danger, people have tried crossing in various ways, including skiing, kayaking, rowing, and even flying in a microlight plane. You and your companions decide on a combination of walking and swimming.

PACKING UP

• Pack your food, clothes, and equipment on a sled. You will need a GPS (Global Positioning System) unit for keeping track of where you are, and a satellite phone for keeping in touch with your support team and finding out about the weather conditions ahead. You need to wear a dry suit (a full bodysuit with rubber seals at the wrists and neck) to keep the freezing water out. You will also need a life jacket, an ice axe (see page 34), a good tent, and a sleeping bag.

WALKING ON THIN ICE

• Pick your way over the ice. Look for the largest, flattest piece of ice you can find and walk, dragging your sled behind you for as long as you can. Listen for grinding, groaning, howling, and screeching sounds, which warn you that the ice is melting. Strong currents and winds in the Bering Strait can cause leads (channels of water) to open up suddenly, stopping you in your tracks.

• When it gets too dark to continue, find the most stable piece of ice you can and pitch your tent on it. Stay away from the edge. Before getting into your sleeping bag, line it with

something called a vapor barrier, which is like a large plastic bag. This will stop moisture from your body freezing inside your sleeping bag and filling it with ice.

• Be prepared for lots of setbacks. If the wind picks up, drifting ice can carry you in the opposite direction of the one you want to take. It can be very disconcerting to wake up in the morning to find you have drifted miles off course. This is where your GPS comes in handy. Use it to keep track of where you should be heading.

TAKING THE PLUNGE

• If a lead opens up in front of you, you have no choice but to get in and swim. Be careful—the water is freezing and up to 50 yards deep. Your dry suit should keep you dry, but try to be in the water for as short a time as possible. Jump in and

start swimming, pulling your sled behind you. When you reach the other side, use your ice axe to pull yourself up onto the ice.

• Apart from the freezing temperatures, strong currents, and changeable weather, keep an eye out for hungry polar bears. They are known to live out on the ice. They usually feed on seals, but when food is scarce, they wouldn't turn their nose up at an explorer for supper. If all else fails, use your satellite phone to call for a rescue helicopter to come to your aid.

HOW TO BATTLE THROUGH A BLIZZARD IN ANTARCTICA

You land in Antarctica in the middle of winter. It is bitterly cold, with howling winds. You're surrounded by ice as far as the eye can see. You are here on a mission to study a colony of emperor penguins and these hardy birds breed in winter on the Antarctic ice. Just as you leave your tent to start the long journey to the colony, a blizzard blows up. You are in danger.

A blizzard is an extremely dangerous winter storm in which strong winds whip up the surface snow and blow it along. Unfortunately

for you, Antarctica is one of the windiest places on Earth and blizzards strike suddenly and frequently. The worst type of blizzard is called a whiteout and that's what you find yourself in now. During a whiteout, visibility is reduced to zero and everything looks the same—white—so you can't tell the ground from the sky. You find yourself being blasted by thick clouds of swirling snow that make it hard to hear and breathe. The blizzard might blow over quickly, but severe blizzards can last for a week. To have any chance of surviving, you need to stay calm and follow some basic safety tips.

BLIZZARD SURVIVAL TIPS

• If you are inside your tent when the blizzard strikes, sit it out and wait for it to blow over. If you have to go outside, tie one end of a long rope to your tent and the other end to you. It is very easy to lose your bearings in a blizzard and this way you will be able to find your way back. Be careful—the wind can be strong enough to knock you off your feet.

• If you are stranded outside, keep your mouth covered so you don't swallow too much snow and suffocate. This cover will also protect your lungs from breathing bitterly cold air.

• Try to find some shelter. The longer you are out in the cold, the greater your risk of getting hypothermia (see page 37) or frostbite. Dig a cave or trench in the snow to protect you from the wind (see page 47).

• If the wind is so strong you can't pitch your tent, make a wind barrier from sleds or backpacks, and shelter behind it. Wrap yourself in your tent or sleeping bag.

• Don't eat snow, even if you are thirsty. It lowers your body temperature and makes you feel even colder. Melt the snow first. You need to drink plenty of water to avoid getting dehydrated.

AVOIDING FROSTBITE

Frostbite is another hazard you face in Antarctica. It happens when parts of your body, especially your fingers, nose, ears, cheeks, chin, and toes, get so cold that they freeze. It damages your body permanently and may lead to affected toes and fingers having to be amputated (cut off).

• Watch for your skin turning red. It may start to tingle before going numb. Alternatively, your skin may look white or yellow, and feel unusually waxy or firm. These are all warning signs that frostbite is beginning.

• Because of the numbness, you may not notice you've got frostbite until someone else points it out to you. Get treatment immediately. Place the affected part in warm (not hot) water to thaw it out or warm it.

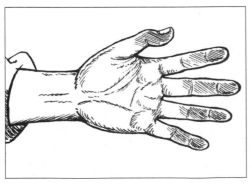

• Never rub or massage the frostbitten parts, and don't use heat lamps or heat pads to warm them up, as the numb skin can easily burn without you realizing. This only makes the damage worse.

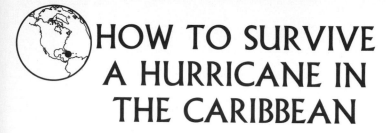

HOW TO SURVIVE A HURRICANE IN THE CARIBBEAN

After hot-footing it all around the world, what better way to relax than having a nice, long holiday in the sun? You are on the island of Grenada in the Caribbean. You have chosen this island for its long, white sandy beaches and warm tropical climate.

One morning while enjoying your breakfast, you hear over the radio that a hurricane is on its way and people are being warned to prepare themselves. You ask the hotel tour guide, Leah, what this means and what you should do.

HOW HURRICANES HAPPEN

Leah tells you that hurricanes are big circular winds. They are caused by the sea warming the air above. This warm air rises high into the sky, taking water vapor up with it. As this warm air rises, cold air rushes in to take its place, causing strong winds. As warm air rises it also cools, causing the water vapor to condense into water droplets and form heavy thunderclouds. The air spins in a big circle, getting faster and faster, with winds reaching speeds of up to 155 miles per hour.

Hurricanes are common in the Caribbean between July and October, and they cause a lot of damage. To record the strength of a hurricane, people measure wind speed, and the severity of a hurricane is classified on something called the Saffir-Simpson scale.

THE SAFFIR-SIMPSON SCALE

Category	Wind speed	Damage
One	74–95 miles per hour	Slight damage to trees, signs, and mobile homes.
Two	96–110 miles per hour	Slight damage to roofs, piers, and doors. Some trees blown down.
Three	111–130 miles per hour	Severe damage to windows, doors, and roofs. Flooding along the coast.
Four	131–155 miles per hour	Some buildings and all trees and signs blown down. Mobile homes destroyed. Risk of all areas below 10 feet above sea level flooding.
Five	more than 155 miles per hour	Many roofs blown off completely. Severe damage to homes and buildings. Widespread flooding.

BATTENING DOWN THE HATCHES

Leah asks if you will help clear everything away to save it from being damaged. Together, you gather up all the furniture by the pool and around the snack bar and move it indoors. Windows and storm shutters are closed and locked, and windows without shutters are boarded up to protect them from flying debris. If windows are left open during a hurricane, the wind can blow in and can cause the air pressure in the house to be so high that the roof blows off.

Once you have secured everything you can, Leah says that it is no longer safe to be outside because the wind has picked up and the sky is getting very dark. You go indoors into the dining room of the hotel with the rest of the guests. This room is ideal because it is an interior room with no windows so there is no shattered glass to blow in.

THERE SHE BLOWS

As you all shelter in the dining room, you can hear the wind blowing very hard outside and howling around the building. It gets louder and louder so that you can hardly hear what people are saying. It seems to last a very long time. Then everything gets very quiet. Phew…you think the storm is over, but Leah tells you to stay where you are. She says that you are just in the eye of the storm, an area in the center of the swirling hurricane where there is very little rain and wind. Once the eye has passed, there will be more to come.

You all stay where you are, and soon you hear the winds picking up again as loudly as before. The storm continues throughout the night and despite the noise, you manage to get some sleep.

THE DAMAGE

In the morning, everything in the dining room is very quiet as people start to wake up. The hurricane has passed and you all make your way out of the building to see what has been damaged. Trees have been blown down and the roofs of some of the outbuildings are very badly damaged. The windows with shutters seem to be OK, but many of the boards have come off the ones without them and the glass has blown in.

Leah says you have been very lucky and that the damage is not that bad this time. It can be much worse—whole villages and towns have been destroyed and many people have been killed, injured, or left without homes for many months until everything is cleared up.

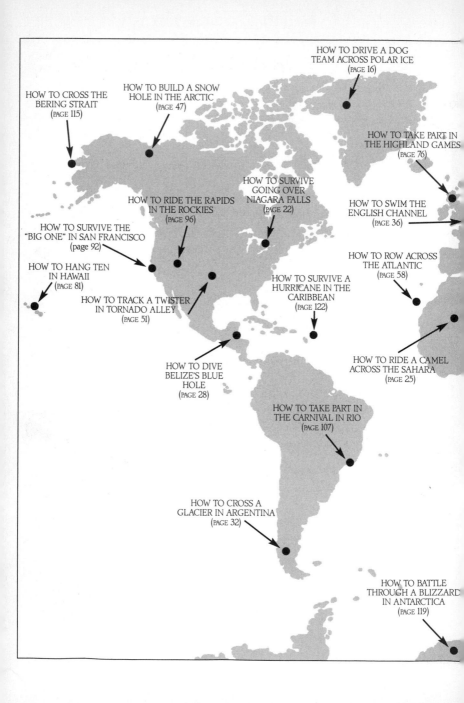

HOW TO DRIVE A DOG
TEAM ACROSS POLAR ICE
(PAGE 16)

HOW TO BUILD A SNOW
HOLE IN THE ARCTIC
(PAGE 47)

HOW TO CROSS THE
BERING STRAIT
(PAGE 115)

HOW TO TAKE PART IN
THE HIGHLAND GAMES
(PAGE 76)

HOW TO SURVIVE
GOING OVER
NIAGARA FALLS
(PAGE 22)

HOW TO RIDE THE RAPIDS
IN THE ROCKIES
(PAGE 96)

HOW TO SWIM THE
ENGLISH CHANNEL
(PAGE 36)

HOW TO SURVIVE THE
"BIG ONE" IN SAN FRANCISCO
(page 92)

HOW TO ROW ACROSS
THE ATLANTIC
(PAGE 58)

HOW TO HANG TEN
IN HAWAII
(PAGE 81)

HOW TO SURVIVE A
HURRICANE IN THE
CARIBBEAN
(PAGE 122)

HOW TO TRACK A TWISTER
IN TORNADO ALLEY
(PAGE 51)

HOW TO RIDE A CAMEL
ACROSS THE SAHARA
(PAGE 25)

HOW TO DIVE
BELIZE'S BLUE
HOLE
(PAGE 28)

HOW TO TAKE PART IN
THE CARNIVAL IN RIO
(PAGE 107)

HOW TO CROSS A
GLACIER IN ARGENTINA
(PAGE 32)

HOW TO BATTLE
THROUGH A BLIZZARD
IN ANTARCTICA
(PAGE 119)

WHERE IN THE WORLD?

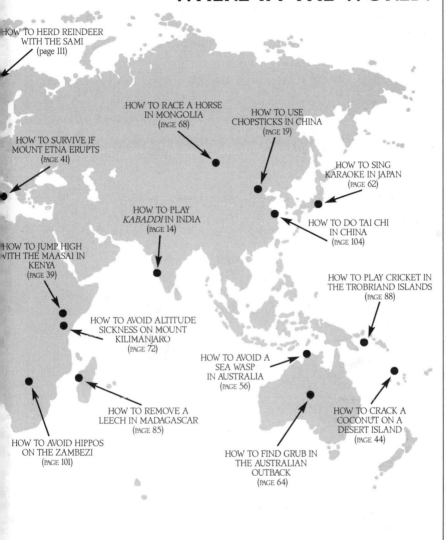

HOW TO HERD REINDEER
WITH THE SAMI
(page 111)

HOW TO RACE A HORSE
IN MONGOLIA
(PAGE 68)

HOW TO USE
CHOPSTICKS IN CHINA
(PAGE 19)

HOW TO SURVIVE IF
MOUNT ETNA ERUPTS
(PAGE 41)

HOW TO SING
KARAOKE IN JAPAN
(PAGE 62)

HOW TO PLAY
KABADDI IN INDIA
(PAGE 14)

HOW TO DO TAI CHI
IN CHINA
(PAGE 104)

HOW TO JUMP HIGH
WITH THE MAASAI IN
KENYA
(PAGE 39)

HOW TO PLAY CRICKET IN
THE TROBRIAND ISLANDS
(PAGE 88)

HOW TO AVOID ALTITUDE
SICKNESS ON MOUNT
KILIMANJARO
(PAGE 72)

HOW TO AVOID A
SEA WASP
IN AUSTRALIA
(PAGE 56)

HOW TO REMOVE A
LEECH IN MADAGASCAR
(PAGE 85)

HOW TO CRACK A
COCONUT ON A
DESERT ISLAND
(PAGE 44)

HOW TO AVOID HIPPOS
ON THE ZAMBEZI
(PAGE 101)

HOW TO FIND GRUB IN
THE AUSTRALIAN
OUTBACK
(PAGE 64)